No. 12 in the BMH Discussion Series

THE INSPIRATION OF THE BIBLE

ALVA J. McCLAIN

THE INSPIRATION OF THE BIBLE

ALVA J. McCLAIN
Founder and First President,
Grace Theological Seminary

BMH Books
Winona Lake, Indiana 46590

Cover photo by Camerique
    Design by Mary Jane Fretz

ISBN: 0-88469-115-2

COPYRIGHT 1965
BMH BOOKS
WINONA LAKE, INDIANA

Printed in U.S.A.

First printing, June 1965
Second printing, January 1983

THE INSPIRATION OF THE BIBLE

By Alva J. McClain

Any attempt to discuss the inspiration of the Bible involves the consideration of three questions:

First—Is the Bible inspired?

Second—What is the nature of its inspiration?

Third—What is the extent of its inspiration?

The first of these questions is, of course, nontechnical, and there is general agreement as to its answer. It is probably no exaggeration to say that if this question should be put to 1,000 intelligent, educated men selected at random, 900 of them would answer without hesitation, "Yes, the Bible is inspired." Thus far there is general unity.

The other two questions are not so easily settled. Suppose we go to these men who believe the Bible is inspired, and ask of them, "What do you mean by *inspired*? What *kind* of inspiration is it, and how far does it *extend*?" At once our beautiful unity is shattered, and a multitude of conflicting voices are lifted up in defense of the various theories of inspiration. To enumerate and discuss all these theories would be a task beyond the scope of this booklet. But several of them deserve mention as an introduction to our subject.

(1) The *ordinary* theory: God influenced the writers of Scripture as He influenced Tennyson and other great writers. This theory degrades inspiration to the level of mere human genius.

(2) The *limited* theory: Parts of the Bible are inspired. The Bible is not the Word of God. It only contains the Word of God. This theory is worthless! Who is competent to inform us which parts are inspired and which are not?

(3) The *degrees* theory: Some parts of the Bible are more inspired than others. This theory is impossible. Truth is not subject to degrees. A thing is either true or not true.

(4) The *dynamic* theory: The material is of God, the form is of men. The thoughts are of God, the words are of men. This theory is unscientific. Thoughts cannot be expressed apart from words.

(5) The *moral* theory: The moral and spiritual teaching of the Bible is inspired; the historical element may or may not be true. This theory is inconsistent. If the Bible may be mistaken in "earthly things," how can we trust it to speak about "heavenly things"?

(6) The *mechanical* theory: The Bible writers were mere machines through which God dictated the Scriptures. This has an element of truth, but it ignores the facts and betrays ignorance of God's methods. His working is never mechanical.

All these theories of inspiration, if not positively erroneous, are at least *inadequate* to explain the Bible. The wise method is to put them all aside and formulate our doctrine as we consider the testimony of the Book itself.

I. IS THE BIBLE INSPIRED?

The lines of proof for the inspiration of the Bible are numerous and convincing. There is its marvelous *unity,* unexplainable apart from the divine authorship. There is its righteous *character,* giving it indeed a right to be called "the Good Book." There is its transforming *power,* as evidenced in the lives of men and nations. There is its consciousness of *authority,* unparalleled in any merely human book. There is its mysterious *indestructibility,* a link which surely binds it to God, "who only hath immortality." Besides all this, we have strong proof for the inspiration of the Bible in its *fulfilled prophecy,* in its *scientific accuracies,* and in that latest but not least of the biblical sciences—*archaeology.* Taken alone, each one of these lines of proof constitutes a powerful argument. When taken together, they are overwhelming and unanswerable.

In my estimation, however, the crowning proof of inspiration is not among these already mentioned. I am a Christian, and to us who are Christians there is one voice above all—a voice that is final. That voice is the voice of the "Son of God who loved us and gave himself for us!" I am willing gratefully to employ all the resources of a reverent textual criticism in order that I may know exactly what He said. But when I find what He said, upon any subject whatever, that to me is *truth!* Therefore, when I find what Christ thought about the Scriptures, that is what I must think about the Scriptures, for "the servant is not greater than his Lord; neither he that is sent greater than he that sent him" (John 13:16).

What, then, did Christ think about the Scriptures? The first thing that will strike the careful reader of the Gospels is our Lord's constant *reference* to the Scriptures. These references seem to cover the whole period of history recorded in the Old Testament. He speaks of man's creation, the institution of marriage, the death of Abel, the days of Noah, the Flood, the destruction of Sodom, the history of Abraham, the appearing of Jehovah in the burning bush, the manna from heaven, the lifting up of the brazen serpent, the life of David, the glory of Solomon, the ministry of Elijah, the sign of Jonah, and the martyrdom of Zechariah. Besides these references, we find Him continually *quoting* from the Scriptures. Over and over from His lips we hear the formula, "It is written!" Still further, if we study the Gospels closely, we shall be amazed at the number of His *indirect allusions* to the Old Testament. He knew the Scriptures as no other one has ever known them. His mind, His memory, His speech, were saturated with the Scriptures. Yet in all the record we have of His words, there is not the slightest intimation that the Scriptures may be untrustworthy at any point. Can we not, therefore, with appropriateness quote the Lord's own word here: "If it were not so, I would have told you" (John 14:2)?

But let us examine a few specific instances of our Lord's reference to Scripture. There are so many it is difficult to choose.

When the time arrives for Him to begin His public ministry, He finds in Isaiah 61 the prophecy which announced it, and declares, "This day is this scripture fulfilled" (Luke 4:21).

When the cities where He preaches refuse to hear the message, He reminds them of the awful fate of Sodom and Gomorrah (Matt. 11:20-22).

Speaking to Nicodemus about the kingdom of God, He declares that "As Moses lifted up the serpent in the wilderness, even so must the Son of man be lifted up" (John 3:14).

If the Pharisees demand a sign, He points to the much ridiculed experience of Jonah and declares nothing further shall be given (Matt. 12:39).

When the disciples come asking about His second coming and the end of the age, He answers with a prophecy from Joel, another from Daniel, an illustration from Genesis, and concludes by saying, "Remember Lot's wife" (Luke 17:32).

When the Sadducees come with their astonishing argument against the resurrection, He confutes them by finding continuity of life after death in the present tense of a verb understood in the Book of Exodus. And He points to the source of their blunder as "not knowing the scriptures" (Matt. 22:23-32).

When the Jews are about to stone Him for blasphemy because He called Himself the Son of God, He quotes in self-defense an obscure passage from the Psalms and reminds them of what they all admitted, that "the scripture cannot be broken" (John 10:33-36).

When Peter draws the sword to defend Him from the mob who sought His life, this impulsive disciple is sternly rebuked with a reminder that all those things written in the "scriptures" must be fulfilled (Matt. 26:52-54).

After His resurrection He finds two disciples on their way to Emmaus. He might have turned their despair instantly into joy by simply saying, "It is I." But, instead, He begins at Moses and all the prophets to show them the things written concerning Himself. Their faith must rest upon the written Word (Luke 24:27).

While hanging on the cross, our Lord had seen Scripture after Scripture fulfilled. The sheep had been scattered. He was left alone with no comforters. His hands and feet were pierced. His bones were out of joint. His garments were parted. Lots were cast for His vesture. At this point John, as an eyewitness, writes, "Jesus knowing that all things were now accomplished, that the scripture might be fulfilled, saith, *I thirst*" (John 19:28). Why did our Lord say that? Certainly there was the physical necessity. But there was another necessity. In Psalm 69 it had been written, "In my thirst they gave me vinegar to drink" (v. 21). And He could not die until that was fulfilled! This is the doctrine of inspiration we learn at the cross. These modern theories of inspiration which dishonor the Bible were not formulated in the shadow of the cross.

Thus far all the testimony of Christ we have considered has been concerning the Old Testament. What about the New Testament Scriptures? Not one page of them was written while our Lord was upon earth, as far as we know. To this it may be answered that if Jesus Christ be the eternal Son of God, He is competent as a witness to the inspiration of Scripture even before it is written. To deny this is to deny His divine Sonship. While upon earth Christ plainly declared He was leaving revelation unfinished: "I have many things to say unto you, but ye cannot bear them now" (John 16:12). He also promised that revelation would be completed when the Holy Spirit was "come" (John 16:13). He therefore chose certain men through whom to make this revelation and gave to their words all the authority of His own (John 15:16, 26-27). He even foretold the content of the New Testament revelation. The Holy Spirit would bring to their "remembrance" things which were past (John 14:26). He would show unto them the things of Christ (John 16:14-15). He would declare unto them "things to come" and guide them into "all truth" (John 16:13). Thus New Testament revelation, as outlined beforehand by Christ, would be *historical, doctrinal, prophetical,* and *final.* I need not point out that our New Testament is exactly this.

Now our examination of Christ's testimony has been only partial and superficial, but it has been sufficient to reveal His estimate of the Scriptures. To Him, Scripture was the infallible and eternal Word of God, of which not one statement nor word can possibly be broken, the final court beyond which there is no appeal. This is the mind of Christ, according to His recorded testimony, and most Christians will be content to follow the apostolic injunction, "Have this mind in you which was also in Christ Jesus" (Phil. 2:5 ASV).

No man has ever successfully disputed the fact that our Lord's recorded testimony supports the most absolute doctrine of inspiration. The only alternative left for dissenters is to advance certain theories which are intended to destroy the value of His testimony. Of these theories I shall mention two.

First, there is the *"accommodation* theory." According to this theory, Christ knew the Scriptures were filled with errors, but because the people to whom He spoke believed the Scripture could not be broken, therefore He *accommodated* His teaching to their ideas in order to give no offense. This reduces our Lord to the level of a second-rate politician, and will be rejected by every loyal Christian as viciously false to all we know about Him. He corrected the errors of mankind instead of acquiescing in them (Matt. 22:30).

Another popular theory is the "*kenosis* theory." This takes its stand upon the Christological statement in Philippians 2:7 (ASV) and contends that Christ, at His entrance into the world, "emptied himself," among other things, of His omniscience, thus becoming, as a man, liable to the mistaken notions of His day. An adequate discussion of this theory is, of course, impossible in our limited space. But this much may be said: We can admit there was some sort of true "kenosis" or "self-limitation" involved in the incarnation without at all admitting the wild conclusions drawn from it. In the first place, *limited knowledge does not necessarily involve the teaching of error.* Granted our Lord knew not the hour of His return, let us at least give Him credit for never attempting to set the date of it! Even here He is the infallible Teacher! We could wish that some of His professed followers might so emulate His example as to teach only those things of which they are sure. In the second place, *our Lord claimed infallibility in all that He taught,* solemnly reminding those who heard, "He that rejecteth me, and receiveth not my words, hath one that judgeth him: the word that I have spoken, the same shall judge him in the last day. For I have not spoken of myself; but the Father which sent me, he gave me a commandment, what I should say, and what I should speak" (John 12:48-49). "I do always those things that please him" (John 8:29). In the light of these words, the very "kenosis" of Christ becomes the guarantee of His infallibility! For He "emptied himself" to become a bondservant, to be the perfect example of what a bondservant should be! But, as Bishop Moule has pointed out, a perfect bondservant must render a perfect bondservice. He must act and speak always in accordance with the will of him that sent him. Is any Christian so rash as to say that Christ failed here? His challenge has stood for eighteen centuries, "Which of you convinceth me of sin? And if I say the truth, why do ye not believe me?" (John 8:46). I repeat, therefore, the kenosis of our Lord, whatever the precise nature of it was, does not make Him the fallible creature of the "destructive criticism." It is rather the guarantee of His infallibility!

II. WHAT IS THE NATURE OF INSPIRATION?

Here I wish to emphasize two distinctions which have been pointed out by different writers, among whom we should mention Kuyper, Hodge, and Gray.

First, *inspiration is not merely a heightened form of spiritual illumination.* Such illumination is common to all Christians, is subject to degrees, and has always been continuous to some extent. But inspiration is not common to all Christians, is never subject to degrees, and most certainly has not been continuous. The fact of the matter is that no Scripture has been written for 1,800 years. Those who contend that inspiration is nothing more than spiritual illumination should demonstrate their theory by writing some Scripture for us!

Second, *inspiration is not even revelation in the strict sense of that term.* Revelation is God's act in communicating divine truth to the human mind. Inspiration is the result of God's act in controlling those who impart this revelation to others. As Chalmers put it, the one is an inflowing; the other is an outflowing. I am inclined to believe that the failure to distinguish properly between revelation and inspiration has been the chief source of many theories on the subject of inspiration. It is said, for instance, that the Ten Commandments are more inspired than the story of the Exodus, because Jehovah gave the Ten Commandments and the Exodus was only a historical event which Moses knew without special revelation. But the method by which a writer of Scripture secured his information is never the measure of its inspiration. God has many and various methods of revealing truth to men. He spoke face to face with Moses, to Daniel in visions, to Joseph in a dream, to Paul directly by the Holy Spirit. At other times, revelation was given in historical events. Here is a great mass of revelation, given at different times and in various ways (Heb. 1:1). The problem was to get this revelation before the world accurately and in permanent form. To do this necessitated a divine act in so influencing certain men that they would select the right material and record it with infallible accuracy. The result of this divine act gave to the world an inspired Bible.

The nearest approach, perhaps, to a definition of inspiration is found in 2 Timothy 3:16. Here we are told that "all scripture is given by inspiration of God." Warfield has pointed out, the English word "inspiration" is really a misnomer for the thing we are discussing. But it has become so firmly entrenched in our theological language that we shall probably never get rid of it. To say that Scripture is *in*-spired of God gives the impression that Scripture is something already existing, *into* which God breathed. Paul did not say this. He said, "All Scripture is *theopneustos—Godbreathed!*" That is to say, all Scripture is the product of the creative breath of God! No stronger term could have been chosen to assert the divine authorship of Scripture. The "breath of God" in the Bible is a symbol of His almighty, creative Word. So we are told the heavens were made "by the *breath* of his mouth . . . he spake, and it was done" (Ps. 33:6, 9). Into the first man, God "*breathed* . . . the breath of life; and man became a living soul" (Gen. 2:7). To say, therefore, that Scripture is "God-breathed" is to place the Scriptures in the same category as the universe and the spirit of man. All three are "God-breathed," the direct product of Almighty God.

All this makes it plain that the object of what we call "inspiration" is not the *man*, but the *Book*; not the writer, but his writings; not the speaker, but his words. The purpose of God in inspiration was not to give us a number of infallible men who would soon pass away, but to give us an infallible Book which would never pass away. As the prophet said, "All flesh is grass . . . the grass withereth, the flower fadeth: but the word of our God shall stand for ever" (Isa. 40:6-8). Flesh may fail and pass away, but the Word stands. Here is the dividing line—the great gulf fixed between most theories of inspiration and the truth. Theories look at the writers. The truth looks at the Book. Theories say, "Matthew, Mark and John were inspired." The truth says, "The Scriptures are inspired."

It is also evident that inspiration describes a *result* rather than a *process.* How God could control a man so that what he wrote would be the very Word of God is an inscrutable mystery, and I venture to say it will always remain so. But why should such a question concern us? What we need to know is not, "*How* did God breathe forth the Scriptures?" but "Did He do it?" When we are hungry the thing that interests us most is that there is food on the table. How the different dishes were made we are willing to leave with the cook. How the different elements were combined so as to make food, we are willing to leave to the savants. Let them discuss it. We shall eat. So to the Christian it is enough to know that the Scripture is God-breathed. He will feed upon it as the living Word of the living God and let the doctors wrangle over how it came to be so. I suppose that the *process* of inspiration will always be a field of legitimate inquiry, but it is the *result* that interests me most. It is better to have life than to be able to explain life. It is better to know the Scriptures are God-breathed than to know how it was done!

III. WHAT IS THE EXTENT OF THE BIBLE'S INSPIRATION?

How far did God exercise His influence over the writers of Scripture? Did it extend only to the *thoughts* and *ideas* expressed, or did it extend down even to the choice of their *words*? On this point the Bible bears no uncertain witness. The words of Scripture are inspired. Out of the mass of testimony we shall select only three references:

(1) "All scripture is God-breathed" (2 Tim. 3:16). But Scripture is *"graphe"*—writing! And writing is impossible without words.

(2) Writing to the Corinthians, the Apostle Paul declares he speaks "not in the words which man's wisdom teaches, but [in words] which the Holy Ghost teacheth" (1 Cor. 2:13).

(3) The testimony of our Lord is not less definite, but really advances far beyond all other declarations on this point. He reminds His hearers that heaven and earth might pass away, but not "one *jot* or one *tittle*" could in any wise pass away from the law "till all be fulfilled" (Matt. 5:18).

An inspired Bible apart from inspired words is an unthinkable, absurd proposition. There is but one kind of biblical inspiration, and that is *verbal* inspiration. For no matter what your particular theory may be, it has to do with *words*. The Bible is a Book of words! Take away the words and you have nothing left but the paper.

"No," someone may say, "we have more than that. We have the thoughts of the Bible left, and *they* are inspired."

This is a statement which can easily be tested. Show me a biblical thought apart from its words! Yes, I know you might dramatize a thought and thus show it to me. But where and how did you get your thought? There is but one answer—the *Bible!* It may be fascinating for some to ride these metaphysical merry-go-rounds, but when the thing stops and we get off, we are back to *words* every time!

The doctrine of verbal inspiration has been severely criticized on the grounds that it is mechanical, degrades the writers to the level of mere machines, and leaves no room for free-agency! This criticism is unfair and reveals an ignorance, not only of the thing criticized, but also of the nature of free-agency. But suppose the criticism were based on fact. Even then we might well reply in the words of another: "The accuracy of God's revelation is a thing vastly more important than the free-agency of a few men!" But the doctrine of a verbally inspired Bible does not rob its writers of their free-agency. The ultimate aim of every Christian is to be controlled by the Holy Spirit, in thought and word and deed. If this means a loss of our free-agency, then we are all working toward a goal which will make us nothing but machines. How foolish! To be Spirit-controlled does not mean the loss of free-agency. A free agent acts as he pleases, and the Spirit-controlled man pleases to act in accordance with the mind of the Spirit. There is nothing at all mechanical about it. Furthermore, the very men who object to the idea of inspired words are willing to endorse the idea of inspired thoughts. They seem to feel that God could control the *thoughts* of man without violating his free-agency, but not his *words!* Here we might ask with Dr. Gray, "Where does the free-agency of man reside; in his mind or in his mouth?" Shall we say that man is free when God controls his thoughts, but he is not free when that control extends to the expression of his thoughts? The whole argument is well summed up by A. J. Gordon, who remarks: "To deny the Holy Spirit speaks in Scripture is an intelligible proposition. But to admit that He speaks, then it is impossible for us to know what He says except as we have His words."

Certainly it must always be remembered that when we speak of the inspiration of the words of Scripture, we logically mean those words which were written by Paul, Moses, and others. To this it has been replied that the documents written by Paul and Moses have perished. Why contend for the inspiration of something we do not possess? Here it is well to remind the objector that the same question might also be asked of those who believe in *any* kind of biblical inspiration. But there is an answer. Granted the original documents are lost, the *words* of those documents are still with us through copies made before their loss. And insofar as we have these words, we have a verbally inspired Bible today. The whole science of textual criticism proceeds upon the assumption of an inspired original. And we cannot honor too highly that company of godly scholars who have labored to lead us back to this original.

Verbal inspiration does not deny there is a human element

in Scripture. Or perhaps it would be more exact to speak of it as a human *aspect*. Every book bears the imprint of the human writer. Who has not felt the "human touch" as Paul asks for "the cloke that I left at Troas . . . the books, but especially the parchments"? Or in 1,000 other instances? The Bible is the most human book in the world! That is one reason why people love it! But this does not make void the Bible's divinity and infallibility! Human things are not necessarily fallible or false. We have gotten that idea from observing a sinful humanity. But let us contemplate our Lord Jesus Christ. He was human, in the only true sense of the word. Yet He is divine, sinless, and never wrong. He was the *Truth*. So the Bible is the most human Book in the world, yet it always speaks with divine authority and with infallible accuracy.

Difficulties with this doctrine there may be, but they are only such as might be expected. When we refuse to accept a doctrine of Christianity because we cannot immediately solve all its difficulties, we shall probably cease to be Christian.* What man has ever solved all the problems of the triune God, or the incarnation of Christ? Besides, *no* theory of inspiration has ever been advanced without its difficulties. And the doctrine of verbal inspiration has this tremendous advantage: *It is based upon the testimony of our Lord and the Book itself.*

I conclude with the beautiful figure of Gaussen. You have watched the skillful musician place his fingers upon the keyboard of the organ. And then you have heard the whispering of the winds, the crash and thunder of the storm, the tramp of armies, the chiming of the bells, and perhaps the sobbing as of a heart torn with grief. Is the eternal God less a genius than man? To sound forth His revelation, He used a human keyboard extending over sixty centuries. When He chose to reveal the coming of the only begotten Son into the world, He laid His right hand upon Enoch, the seventh from Adam, and His left hand upon John, the weary exile of Patmos. The celestial hymn be-

---

*See *The "Problems" of Verbal Inspiration* by Alva J. McClain.

gan with Enoch, "Behold, the Lord cometh with ten thousands of his saints." And in the eternal harmony of revelation, the voice of John echoes in response, "Behold, he cometh with clouds; and every eye shall see him"!

On this wonderful keyboard we sometimes hear the sublime and untutored simplicity of John. Again, it is the startling argument of Paul; sometimes the fervor and solemnity of Peter, or the majestic poetry of Isaiah, the simple narrative of Moses, the royal wisdom of Solomon. There is no deception here. It was John, and Paul, and Peter, and Isaiah. But, above all, it is *God!*

Additional publications by Dr. Alva J. McClain . . .

The "Problems" of Verbal Inspiration
The Greatness of the Kingdom
Romans, the Gospel of God's Grace
Daniel's Seventy Weeks
Romans Outlined and Summarized
Freemasonry and Christianity
The Jewish Problem
Law and Grace
Bible Truths

Available at your local Christian bookstore or from BMH Books, P.O. Box 544, Winona Lake, IN 46590. (Phone toll-free for information: 1-800-348-2756.)

The BMH Discussion Series

$1.00

Does God Want Christians To Perform Miracles Today?
By John C. Whitcomb.

Did Christ Die Only for the Elect?
By Charles R. Smith.

Christ, Our Pattern and Plan.
By John C. Whitcomb.

Is the United States in Prophecy?
By Herman A. Hoyt.

Demons, Exorcism and the Evangelical.
By John J. Davis.

Can You Know God's Will for Your Life?
By Charles R. Smith.

A Capsule View of the Bible.
By W. Russell Ogden.

The Biblical Pattern for Divine Healing.
By Richard L. Mayhue.

How To Gain Life-Changing Insights from the Book of Books.
By Cyril J. Barber.

The New "Life After Death" Religion.
By Charles R. Smith.

Snatched Before the Storm!
By Richard L. Mayhue.

The Inspiration of the Bible.
By Alva J. McClain.

ISBN: 0-88469-11

P.O. Box 544
Winona Lake, Indiana 46590